Shirtless
Tattoo

Dedication

For Judy, whose faith runs as deep as my doubt.
For Jana, Calli, Mikaela, and Dylan.
I love you guys.

Acknowledgements

Some of these poems have appeared previously in

Northern Prospects, Your Scrivener Press, 1998
    "When You Married Me Did You Know That You'd
    Get Christmas Cards Like This?", [in a riot of leaves],
    [Lord], [since you left], [there's a feeling], [you make
    me feel], [I hang on the cross of your beauty]

Northern Life
    "'Que Sera Sera' Remains A Fundamental Truth Even
    Though Doris Day Did Sing About It"

in touch, University of Toronto Faculty of Education
Department of English
    [men are icebergs]

Shirtless Tattoo

Anthony Armstrong

Your Scrivener Press

Canadian Cataloguing in Publication Data

Armstrong, Anthony, 1950-
    Shirtless tattoo

Poems.
ISBN 1-896350-08-9

    I. Title.

PS8551.R767S55 1999   C811'.54   C99-900466-2
PR9199.3.A542S55 1999

Book design: Laurence Steven
Cover art and design: Terry Pallot

Published by *Your Scrivener Press*
465 Loach's Road, Sudbury, Ontario, Canada, P3E 2R2
scrivener@sympatico.ca
www3.sympatico.ca/scrivener

Contents

Poems from pages 40 to 60 are untitled

A Poem Written At The Vietnam Veterans' Memorial On March 18th 1998

I stand
at the wall
searching
for the name
of my friend,
though I know
the dead
have no use
for names
and cannot
be chained
to tombstones
or walls
by the loops
of engraved
letters.

I stand
unshaven
in a city
where many men
shave twice
a day,
for there are
meetings
and cameras,
but I
have arrived
without appointment
or audience;
the stubble

is like tombstones
rising
from my skin.

The woman
searching near me
wears no perfume,
and in her failure
sniffs the air
that is filled
with the smell
of empty rooms;
she kisses
the wall
and walks away.

I find
the name
of my friend
and place
a finger
against
the curved trench
of the first letter,
half expecting
it to
grip me
like a baby's hand,
but there is nothing
but the stillness of stone,
the silence of tears,
and the breaking
of my heart.

And as I
back away,

a pigeon
flies in
like a helicopter gunship
and strafes the wall —
birdshit
flows
like blood
across his name.

I told him,
"Don't go."
I told him,
"Come to Canada."
But he died
like some
silent
Socrates
for a country
that has known
no golden age.

Corollaries Of The Theory Of Relativity

Corollary #1:
find wood soft enough
use a nail sharp enough
and a feather is a hammer

Corollary #2:
in an expanding universe
the world is wrapped in parting
you fall asleep together
and wake up all alone

Corollary #3:
in a contracting universe
be sure you are well rested
everyone you've dreamed of
is headed for your bedroom

Corollary #4:
fast enough
you're two dimensions
slow enough
you crowd the stars

Death Poem Of Any Western Man

a tree
has fallen
from a leaf

I Was A Zen Master; He Was A Suicide

night,
Yonge Street,
a doorway;
in his hand there is a rose.

night,
Yonge Street,
a doorway;
on his wrist there is a slash.

but Yonge Street is a rosary of suicides;
it removes me just like some eastern prayer;
and though I rip my tee shirt
and bind the rose to the slash,
it's just as true
I wasn't even there.

Execution By Lethal Injection
And Other Signs Of The Christmas Season
In Texas

while I listened
to my daughter
playing the piano

while houses glowed
in the glitz
of Christmas garters

while George Bush Junior
forgot that God Junior
was ever born

a man
became a worm
washed onto the sidewalk

his love
became a lightbulb
shattered in the socket

his dreams
became matchsticks
snapping as he struck them

and December 8
6:24 p.m.
Jeff Emery
left Texas

Far Then Further

stopping
at The Roastery

drinking
strong coffee

imagining
you there

filling
the chair
opposite me

until somebody says,
"is that chair taken?"

stopping
at The Roastery

drinking
strong coffee

imagining
a chair

First Entry In My Death Journal

there was a butterfly
on the trail

I could not tell
if it was living
or dead

I placed
it on
my palm
and knew
that it
was dead

I let
it fall
back to
the trail
and its wings
fluttered
in a breeze
I could
not feel

Five Card Stud

not much of a fighter
so I spent
the night
on a park bench
and used
my bleeding arm
as a pillow

not much of a lover
if I count
the beds
I've been to
then the ones
I've been to
twice

not much of a husband
for I've been
to Paris
by myself
and often eat
alone

not much of a father
when I fear
a hug's
a species thing

not much of a poker player
unless
I'm bluffing now

beneath the muscle of moon
we lay on the beach
and moved there
like we were the tide

and the sand it mixed in
with your goosebumps of skin
and the stars
combed their hair in your eyes

and the waves were like wax
but our footprints they vanished
like tracks
that jets leave in the sky

we're a week from the moon
years from the stars
oh
that the past
could be part
of the sky

Like Water

you say
you want truth,
but truth
is like water:
it's the shape
of the sky;
it's the shape
of this glass;
it's the shape
of my mouth.
which truth
do you want?

you say
you want love,
but love
is like water:
it can bathe you;
it can cool you;
it can drown you.
which love
do you want?

you say
you want me,
but I
am like water:
I'm a mist;
I'm a splash;
I am ice.
which me
do you want?

you say
you want water,
but water
is like truth;
water
is like love;
water
is like me.
which water
do you want?

My Last Sin

I wanted you

so

I whispered
till you were curious

I hummed
till you sang

I danced
till you tired

I fasted
till you hungered

and then
I did not want you

so

"Que Sera Sera" Remains
A Fundamental Truth Even Though Doris Day
Did Sing About It

she looks up
at me
and says
lover
be happy.

like it was
on the pantry shelf
just behind
the herbal tea,
like it was
an entree
overlooked
on the menu,
like it was
saying
double mushroom
or hold
the MSG.

she looks up
at me
and says
lover
be happy.

like it was
hanging
in the closet
beside

my leather jacket,
like it was
a page
I had not read
in the tour guide,
like it was
found
at every rest stop
on some
spiritual highway.

she looks up
at me
and says
lover
be happy.

as if
I could
have
every woman
I ever
touched
my self with,
as if
there were
a place
I could follow
my prayers to,
as if
the mass
of the mountain
were not
the weight
of dust.

she looks up
at me
and says
lover
be happy.

I look down
at her
and say
lover
be tall.

Queen's Athletic Field

alone
skating
the great oval

knowing
every gash
in the ice
is mine

every
spray
of crystal blood
I made

don't
show me scars
I did
not cause

or photographs
of your
withered lovers

Second Entry In My Death Journal

last night
I was made awake

the darkness was old

there was a pain
inside me

half of it
was in my arm

half of it
was in my chest

I watched it
like a subway passenger
uncertain
of his station

but in the light
of morning
and the face
of my indifference,
the pain
tired
and snaked off
into a tunnel
so dark
I could not tell
if it was shallow
or eternal

several   times   too often
Wide World of Sports
replays
Lee   Harvey   Oswald's   fastball
ripping   through the leather
of JFK's
catcher's mitt
until
it is   no more   to me
than Wyle E. Coyote
fielding   another   anvil
with his head
and I   am early to bed
for tomorrow   I must drive   my car
with its posturepedic mattress
to the Saturn   family   picnic
so I miss   the ex   news   anchor's
late   night   special
on the Home Shopping Network:
for less   than one   dollar   a day
you can feed
a foreign   coloured   child
stomach   pregnant   with emptiness
and receive   letters
thanking   you   and Jesus
in a script   you do not recognize
and a language   you do not understand

oh   I miss
my pocket   radio
that lay   beside   my thirteen year old pillow
and called   me   to exotic

late night   basketball games
in Boston   and New York
until

the tube

made travel

unnecessary

The Awful Rowing
Toward Anne Sexton

I broke
into
the prison
of the highway

where the sun's
just bright
enough
to show
the rain

and the road
took on
the colours
of that sky

till poetry
was the purpose
of my pain

The Potato Prayer

I do not understand
the focus
of Christian prayer

yesterday
I read
The Potato Prayer

now it's fine
to thank god
for anything,
even a potato,

but where
are the sexy prayers?
I want to read
The Orgasm Prayer

but then,
maybe it's just me;
you see
I've never
had a
really
satisfying
potato

What It Is Not And What It Is

it is not
the tap
that drips
like an old flamenco dancer

it is not
the undulation
of kicks
from the chorus line
of a crumbling house

it is not
the repeated chaos
that is the tarantella
of work and commerce

it is
that I dance
at all

for many times
I have travelled
beyond
the halfway point
on a road
that never ends

andtime
aftertime
aftertime
aftertime

I return
to you
and the tap
that drips
like an old flamenco dancer

What I Said When She Asked Me
Why I Drink So Much

truth
is a time

faith
is a place

oh darling
I'm lost

oh lover
I'm late

The Valentine I Never Gave You

I know
that love
and freedom
are merely
grains of sand
upon a beach
that is a fingerprint
of land
that has been
swallowed
by an ocean
that is mist
within a sky
that could not
fill a lung

still,
I love you
and you taste like freedom

When You Married Me, Did You Know That You'd Get Christmas Cards Like This?

Judy says
we have free will;
I say
we have its illusion.

Judy selects
the wine;
I drink
from the bottle,
and tell her
choose to fly.

You can see her
there at the heart
of that gallery of clouds;
she had no choice —
she had to prove me wrong.

Widower's Day

I think of you
sometimes
in the morning
when the islands are dressed
in a negligee of mist

I think of you
sometimes
in the afternoon
when the heat of the day
brings the water to whitecaps

I think of you
sometimes
in the heart of the night
when I stand on the dock
and the stars are in the lake

You've Been Gone So Long
I Doubt You're Ever Coming Back

I have amputated
the hands
of my watch
and strapped
the moon
to my wrist

I have searched
for you
in fractal space
where no
straight lines
exist

my heart
is a broken
satellite
being pulled
to some
abyss

rebel
is a word
my grade seven
teacher
used
on my report card,
but I
was no rebel
for I could not
mask
my terror
as I waited
in the hall
while he found
another teacher
to serve
as witness
to make
the strapping
legal.

communist
is a word
the same teacher
used
to talk about
my poem,
but I
was an eleven year old
Roman Catholic boy
not even allowed
to know

the meaning
of the word
communist;

besides,
if I'd been
a young communist
I'd have grown
into
a machine gun
and mowed
it all down
and started over
in a world
where work
and labour
were equal,
and we'd all
be reimbursed
in the currencies
of sustenance,
privacy,
and time;

but every
revolution
is doomed
to disappoint,
and maybe
I should be
grateful
mine died
before
it started.

Adrift Between Ages

I am adrift
between ages

I lie
beside her
wondering
if she will be the man
and grope me
with her breasts
grab me
with her thighs —
and I'm okay with that

it's the public washrooms
that get me
I stand there
with my hands
beneath the dryer
waiting for the air
that does not come
until I notice
it's an older model
and I have to press the button

and I have heard myself
saying thank you
to an automatic door
and I have seen myself
standing before the old-fashioned kind
waiting for it to open

last night

my answering machine
recorded a message
from an automatic dialing machine
and I was left wondering
"Who's there?"

and I have read
poetry generated by computer
and I have to admit
it is not without value
for if I am ever stranded in the wilderness
and gorge myself on autumn wrinkled berries
and develop stomach cramps that rival Niagara
and find myself without a handful of leaves
I hope I have those poems with me

A butcher
showed me
a way
to use
an embrace
and a blade
with such speed
that the beast
stands amazed,
and death
it arrives
before pain.

It is not much,
but among butchers
it passes for love.

and
when I am gone,
may it be
as a sword withdrawn —
not from a wound
but from a lake

I am walking
out the door
and good-bye
is not even close
to the right word
if there is a word

please,
do not mistake
what I am doing
for leaving
the way you mistook
my presence
after my never having been there
for arriving

I have made love
with three women
who've attempted suicide

two, before they knew me,
never after;
Jane, before she loved me,
and then she loved the razor
in the echo of our laughter

when I remember the two,
I am not the shepherd
and they are not the lost

but when I remember Jane,
my body is a nail
and my bed is the cross

I have not seen the face of god
but I've seen the back of god's head
god's hair was coloured like water
god's skin it was mirrors of lead

I have not seen the face of god
but I've seen the back of god's head
god fell forward into the sand
and when I reached god, god was dead

I want to die
dancing
with some wolf
a throat the only trophy

I want to die
without a breath
between my elemental stiffness
and the rigidity of death

I want to die
the hero discovered naked
the traitor proven right

but let me die tomorrow
The Day the Earth Stood Still
is on the late show tonight

I'm lying
in the tub

a drip
strikes my foot

I cannot tell
if it is hot or cold

you are standing
in the doorway

in a riot of leaves
in a cloud of exhaust
you showed me three ways
to get off a cross:
       like a thief
       like a thief
       and like a perhaps god

now old friends see a phantom
an old lover does too
and I've lost whatever charm it was
that got me to you

but if this is just another cross
I'll be more careful when I choose
until I'm god enough to handle
these resurrection blues

let's be lovers
who meet
like ocean currents
mingling in the
mist above the water

let's be lovers
who part
like the continents
fingers stretching
to kiss beneath the sea

Lord,
am I your child?

then bathe me in a flood,
instruct me with lightning,
age me with your presence;

scare the shit out of me;
I have not knelt in twenty years
and then
it was to a woman.

lover,
when you fear the storm
remember
I'm the one
the wind
is hunting for

it will rip me
from the cradle of your arms
to send me tumbling
cross some desert floor
where jets of air
will pierce me
to the bone

by evening
I'll be porous
by morning
I'll be gone

men are icebergs;
poets are icebergs
who stand on their heads.

I wanted to be a poet
even if I were the only one
holding my breath
as I suggested my soul
to the chemical sun,

but better,
I should find
the fish in my soul,
then I'll learn
to stop talking
and become so holy
I won't have any friends.

my god
is a deadbeat dad

my prayers,
paper planes
of bible pages
hurled
from broken stairs

since you left:

I've committed half a suicide
I've tortured an ocean
I've perfected my limp

I've said two prayers:
I prayed that you'd come back to me
I prayed that you wouldn't

already,
one of my prayers has been answered

the factory
is a cross
where the nails
are so blunt
they
never
break
the skin.

there is
an equation
that marries
cricket
chirps
to temperature

today
I killed
a cricket
with
the front
wheel of
my bicycle

the air
was filled
with music
mournfully
announcing
it's a thousand
degrees

there was a time
when your arms
were my equator

there was a time
I was molded
beneath your cool hand

there was a time
when your lips
created volcanoes

and a time
when ice
flowed like lava
cross this land

there's a feeling
I get in my gut
that tells me
my soul must live there

it's as warm
as the flesh of a tumour
as cold
as the fist of her stare

and on nights such as this
when I feel it
when I'm breathing
both water and air

I curl up
in the lap of confusion
to nurse
at the breast of despair

you are gone

like summer
like Diana in Paris
like a snowy owl in Windsor

the last time you lay beside me
you were a princess,
the white mask of your breasts
disappearing
in the snow
that drifted
across
the fields
of your skin

like those golden dreams
gathered
in the sweep
of the croupier's arm

now,
memories of you
are
aching
wearied
climbers
clinging
to the glacier of my soul

you make me feel
like Mary Magdalene
for there must have been a day
that she came to him with water
when he only wanted shade

and I am sure
he had a parable
that convinced her to remain
but *you*
gave to me a blueprint
and the memory of rain

I hang on the cross of your beauty
I am pinned by my longing for you
my heart is a bird with no legs
my heart is a shirtless tattoo